## Genre Folktale

**Essential Question**
**How can we understand nature?**

WHY TURTLES
LIVE IN WATER

### Retold by Deborah November
### Illustrated by Linda Bittner

**Scene 1**
Life of the Turtle . . . . . . . . . . . . . . . . . . . 2

**Scene 2**
Capture! . . . . . . . . . . . . . . . . . . . . . . . . . . 5

**Scene 3**
The Village . . . . . . . . . . . . . . . . . . . . . . . . 8

**Scene 4**
Escape! . . . . . . . . . . . . . . . . . . . . . . . . . . . 13

**Respond to Reading** . . . . . . . . . . . . . . . . 16

**PAIRED READ** Why Bear Has a Short Tail . . . 17

**Focus on Literary Elements** . . . . . . . . 20

| | |
|---|---|
| Little Turtle | Hunter 1 |
| Turtle Friend 1 | Hunter 2 |
| Turtle Friend 2 | Chief |

SCENE 1

# LIFE OF THE TURTLE

**Setting:** A long time ago in Africa

**Little Turtle:** What a lovely day!

**Turtle Friend 1:** Yes, life is good.

2

**Turtle Friend 2:** We live a happy life playing in the tall grass.

**Little Turtle:** And we always have plenty to eat.

3

**Turtle Friend I:** Some hunters are coming! Hurry and hide!

**Turtle Friend 2:** Little Turtle, run as fast as you can!

STOP AND CHECK

Where do the turtles like to play?

4

# CAPTURE!

**Setting:** A path in the jungle

**Hunter 1:** We have you, Little Turtle!

**Hunter 2:** Don't try to dash away. It is too late.

**Little Turtle:** Oh my goodness! The hunters were so fast I did not even have a chance to holler! I am filled with fear.

**Little Turtle:** I am ashamed that the hunters caught me.

**Hunter I:** No talking, Little Turtle!

STOP AND CHECK

Who caught Little Turtle?

7

# SCENE 3
# THE VILLAGE

**Setting:** The hunters' village

**Hunter 2:** Here we are in our village.

**Little Turtle:** I wonder if their village has similarities to ours!

**Chief:** I am the chief of this village. Welcome, Little Turtle!

**Little Turtle:**
Thank you, Sir!

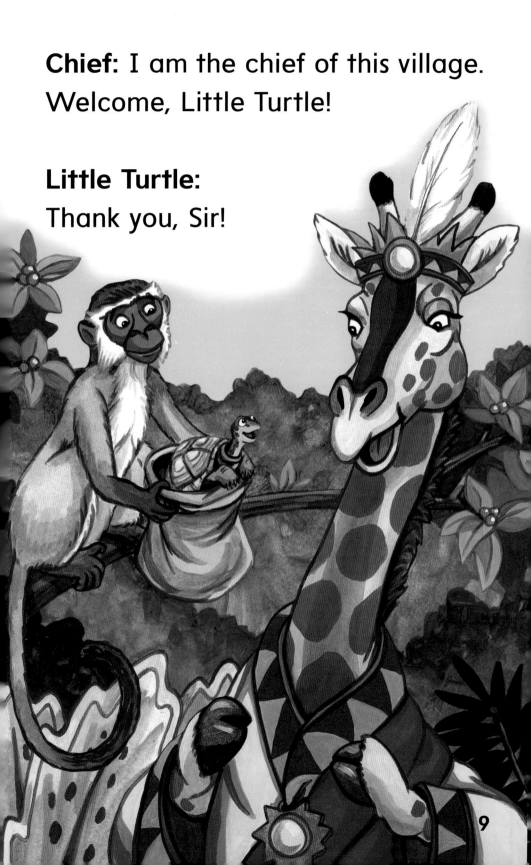

**Chief:** How shall we cook him?

**Little Turtle:** You will have to take me out of this shell.

**Chief:** We'll break your shell with sticks.

**Little Turtle:** You have great wisdom, Chief, but that won't work. Why don't you throw me in the river and drown me?

**Chief:** Good idea, Little Turtle.
Soon we will celebrate our victory.
We will drown the turtle!

STOP AND CHECK

What did the animals of the village want to do to Little Turtle?

# ESCAPE!

**Setting:** The hunters' village

**Little Turtle:** I don't want to boast, but I would not get those cooking pots out too fast!

**Hunter I:** Little Turtle tricked us!

**Chief:** The turtle is getting away!

**Little Turtle:** I think I'll spend most of my time safely in the water from now on.

**Turtle Friend I:** Little Turtle is home and safe!

**Turtle Friend 2:** Let's have a party!

**Turtle Friend I:** And that is why turtles live in water.

STOP AND CHECK

What did Little Turtle say after landing in the river?

15

# Respond to Reading

## Summarize

Use details to summarize *Why Turtles Live in Water.*

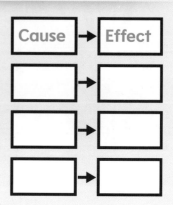

| Cause | | Effect |
|-------|---|--------|
| | → | |
| | → | |
| | → | |

## Text Evidence

1. How do you know *Why Turtles Live in Water* is a folktale? Genre

2. Why did Little Turtle and his friends have a party? Cause and Effect

3. What is the root word of *getting* on page 14? Root Words

4. Write how this folktale explains nature. Write About Reading

**Compare Texts**
Read why bears have short tails.

# Why Bear
## Has a Short Tail

A Flanders Folktale
retold by Jackie Maloy
Illustrated by Sarah Dillard

One day, Bear saw Fox eating
from a pile of fish.

"Where did you get
the fish?" Bear asked.

Fox did not want Bear
to learn she had stolen
the fish. She would play
a trick on Bear.

"I'll show you,"
Fox told Bear.

17

Fox led Bear to a hole in a frozen lake.

"Just put your tail in the hole. Then wait for the fish to bite it," Fox said. "When you feel the bite, pull your tail up. Then you'll have lunch!"

"Great!" said Bear. He sat down and put his tail in the water.

"See you later!" said Fox. She was smiling as she left the lake.

Bear sat waiting for the fish to bite. Before long, the hole froze over. Bear felt his tail trapped in the ice. He tried to pull it out. But when he stood up, his tail stayed in the hole!

"Oh, Fox tricked me!" Bear cried.

Since then, all bears are born with short tails.

## Make Connections
How does Bear lose his tail?
Essential Question

How do these two folktales explain something in nature? Text to Text

# Focus on
# Literary Elements

**Theme** The theme is the lesson or message in a story or play.

**What to Look for** In the play, the author tells you why turtles live in water. Look for what Little Turtle did. How did he end up in the water? What is the lesson?

## Your Turn

Plan a play about an animal. Make a list of details to include in your play. Include where the animal lives. Include how it got its home.